Not All Angels Wear Wings

by

Brenda Thurlbeck

Bloomington, IN  Milton Keynes, UK

AuthorHouse™
1663 Liberty Drive, Suite 200
Bloomington, IN 47403
www.authorhouse.com
Phone: 1-800-839-8640

AuthorHouse™ UK Ltd.
500 Avebury Boulevard
Central Milton Keynes, MK9 2BE
www.authorhouse.co.uk
Phone: 08001974150

© 2006 Brenda Thurlbeck. All rights reserved.

No part of this book may be reproduced, stored in a retrieval system, or transmitted by any means without the written permission of the author.

First published by AuthorHouse 5/4/2006

ISBN: 1-4259-2833-1 (sc)

Printed in the United States of America
Bloomington, Indiana

This book is printed on acid-free paper.

TABLE OF CONTENTS

NOT ALL ANGELS WEAR WINGS..................1
MISSING YOU 2
I KNEW AN ANGEL..4
JUST ONE WISH 5
MOTHER...6
DANCING ON THE MOON 7
COLOURS OF ROSE'S 8
IN A DREAM..9
MY ANGEL...10
THE VISIT 12
ANGELS..14
I PEEKED IN HEAVEN'S GATE.......................15
PHONE HEAVEN 16
MY SOUL MATE 17
I GLIMPSED HEAVEN 18
THE QUESTION 19
THAT SPECIAL SOMEONE................................20
FLOWERS FOR ANGELS 21
MY LOVE..22
NEVER BUY 23
CONTENTMENT...24
IF YOU NEED A FRIEND 26
A BROKEN HEART 27
A LETTER FROM HEAVEN 28
GIFTS 30
TRUE LOVE 31
ONE WISH 32
MAYBE 33
THE ANSWER...34
MIRACLES 35

FRIENDSHIP	36
IN LOVE MANY TIMES	37
LIFES COMPANION	38
FREE WILL	39
GOD'S FLOWER	41
MY FATHER	42
DO YOU BELIEVE	43
LIFE'S PARTNER	44
ASK HIM	46
YOU WALK WITH ME	47
MY CHILD	48
SILVER LINING'S	49
I NEED YOU	51
FINDING GOD	52
A CANDLE	53
TWO SPECIAL PEOPLE	54
FOR A DEAR FRIEND	56
WHITE ROSE'S	57
SEEKING	58
MY HEART	59
JUST GO FOR IT	60
SAFE IN MY HEART	62
LET HIM IN	64
WHY	65
CALL TO HEAVEN	66
FRIEND'S	67
GOD'S ROSE	68
LONELY PEOPLE	70
YESTERDAY	71
A SPECIAL LADY	72
BEAUTY	73
LIFE'S RACE	74

END OF A RAINBOW 75
BOOK OF MEMORIES 76
A GENTLEMAN..78
MY NANA..79
JUST THINK..80
TO MY DAUGHTER 81
GOD'S BLESSING 82
PRAYER'S ANSWERED 83
FLOWERS..84
THANKFUL 85
MEMORY LANE 86
OUR NEW GRANDAUGHTER 87
TO JESSICA MY SPECIAL ANGEL AGE 6
YEARS 88
BUTTERCUPS 89
A PLACE IN HEAVEN 90
A NEW YEAR...92
FAVOURITE FLOWERS.....................................93
HIGHEST PEAK...94
LIFES ROAD 95
RICHES 96
THIS WORLD 97
YOU ARE ALWAYS THERE 98
HOME AGAIN...99
MY SECRET SMILE 100
HEAVEN ON EARTH 101
ONE TUESDAY MORNING 102
MY PRAYER 103
A BIT OF ADVICE 104
HEAVEN 105
DO NOT PRETEND 106
GOD'S LOVE..107

A LETTER ON YOUR BIRTHDAY 108
FOREVER 109
STAR OF HOPE 110
YOU WILL WIN 111
A LETTER TO HEAVEN 113
YESTERDAY..114
THANKYOU...115
THREE LITTLE WORDS 116
OPEN YOU EYES 117
NO DOUBT 118
GOD LOVES US ALL 119
JOURNEY'S END......................................120
GOD PICKED YOU....................................121
ASK GOD 122
DOUBTING THOMAS................................123
SWEET MEMORIES..................................124
SMILE AGAIN 125
TELL HIM 126
PRICELESS 127
MY DREAM...128
ANGEL ON YOUR SHOULDER 129
DREAMS COME TRUE 130
KNOCK ON HEAVEN'S DOOR....................131
WHAT IS LOVE...132

NOT ALL ANGELS WEAR WINGS.

Have you ever seen an angel,
Did you see it's beautiful wings.
Do you think it came from heaven,
Could you feel the pure joy it brings.
Not all angels live in heaven,
Maybe some do not wear wings.
They could be a nurse or a doctor,
Helping others for the satisfaction it brings.
They could be a priest or policeman,
Or a good samariton that picks you up when you fall.
Perhaps a fireman that saves lives,
But i think that the best angels of all,
Are mothers who are raising a family,
Just doing the best they can.
Though life at times is hard for them.,
All mothers have the same plan.
The love that they give cannot be matched,
It is a love you can depend upon.
There will be many other loves in your life,
A mothers love is a special one.
Their childrens happiness is their goal,
They will nourish them until they are grown.
I agree that some angels do wear wings,
But none that i have known.

MISSING YOU

At Night When All Is Silent,
My Eyes Fill Up With Tears.
I Think Of All The Good Times,
Plus All The Happy Years.
If I Could Only See Your Face,
Or I Could Hold You Once Again.
Just To See Your Lovely Smile,
Would Take Away This Pain.
It Is Then I Sense Your Presence,
I Feel Your Tender Touch.
Then I Hear You Whisper,
I Love You Very Much.
Do Not Think That I Have Left You,
I Have Not Travelled Far.
Just Entered God's Beautiful Garden,
And Left The Door Ajar.
I Am Living With The Angels Now,
My Pain And Trials Are Past.
Know My Dearest Loved One,
Our Love Will Always Last.
Remember I Am Only A Thought Away,
I Am Forever In Your Heart.
One Day In God's Good Time,
We Will Never Be Apart.
So Do Not Be Unhappy, Do Not Be Sad,
Just Think Of All The Times To Come,
Think Of All The Years We Had.,
Live For Each Moment,
Make The Most Of Everyday,
Trust In The Dear Lord.

He Will Light Your Way.
Know That I Am Happy, Know That I Care,
And Know That When You Need Me,
I Will Soon Be There.
Some People Just Have Moments,
The Lucky Ones Have Years.
So Dry Your Eyes My Dear One,
Say Goodbye To All Our Tears.

I KNEW AN ANGEL

Once I Knew An Angel,
I Had When I Was Small.
She Gave Me Lots Of Love And Care,
Stayed With Me Until I Grew Tall.
She Was A Gentle Lady,
Who Is In My Thoughts Forever.
Though She Has Gone, She Once Told Me,
That She Would Leave Me Never.
She Taught Me How To Live My Life,
Showed Me How To Care For Others.
Taught Me How To Have Respect.
To Treat Everyone As Brothers.
She Gave Me Love, She Gave Me Faith,
She Gave Me Hope As Well.
Just How Much I Miss Her, I Could Never Tell.
I Often Think Of Bygone Days,
She Loved Me Like No Other,
There Is A Bond Death Cannot Break,
For My Devoted Mother.

JUST ONE WISH

God Gave Ten Men Just One Wish,
To See What They Would Say.
One Asked God For A Warm Coat,
For Days That Were Cold And Grey.
Two Wanted To Be Made A King,
Four Others A Millionaire.
One Wanted Fame And Power,
And One He Did Not Care..
God Thought This World Was Ailing,
His Children Full Of Greed.
If All Are Like These Nine Men,
This World Is Sick Indeed.
One Man Left,what Would He Wish,
God Was Afraid To Guess.
Then A Big Smile Came To God's Face.,
He Just Wanted Happiness.

MOTHER

Memories Like Threads Of Gold,
Just Trickle Through My Mind.
I Try To Think Of Happy Times,
But I So Often Find.
My Thoughts Go Back To Bygone Years,
The Time That We Had To Part.
A Tear Comes To My Eye, A Pain Is In My Heart.
Then My Tears Become A Flood,
My Heart Begins To Break..
I Go To Bed And Try To Sleep,
But I Lie There Wide Awake.
I Cannot Believe That You Are Gone,
A Love That Is Like No Other.
If Only You Were Back Home Again,
My Sweetest, Dearest Mother.

DANCING ON THE MOON

For A Moment I Looked At The Stars,
It Was Then I Thought Of You.
I Wondered If You Were Watching Me,
The Way You Used To Do.
I Saw A Shooting Star So Bright,
That It Lit Up All The Skies.
It Was Then I Thought Of Your Dear Face,
With Your Bright And Sparkling Eyes.
I Made A Wish On That Bright Star,
That You Were There With Me.
I Wished We Could Have One Last Dance,
Along The Galaxy.
I Knew That I Was Not Alone,
I Felt So Close To You.
Your Love Was All Around Me,
A Feeling So Warm And True.
I Walked Into The Garden,
I Could Smell The Flowers Perfume.
You Took Your Hand In My Hand,
Then We Danced Across The Moon.
Too Soon The Music Ended,
The Dawn Began To Break.
I Thought I Had Been Dreaming,
But I Felt Wide Awake.
Another Day Had Started,
Bringing With It Grief And Pain.
I Know When This Day Has Ended,
All The Stars Will Come Out Again.

COLOURS OF ROSE'S

A Man Was Selling Flowers,
On His Flower Stall One Day.
Would You Like Some Rose's,
He Said As He Looked My Way.
What Colour Is Your Favourite,
Red, Yellow, White Or Pink.
As I Turned To Face Him,
His Question Made Me Think.
He Said, Red Is For A Deep Love,
A Love That Is Strong And True.
The Yellow Rose Is A Flower Of Peace,
That Will Cheer Your Heart Up Too.
White Is For Rememberance,
For A Memory Of A Love That Is Gone.
Sweet Pink Is For A Mothers Love,
A Love That Will Go On And On.
There Was A Smile Upon His Face,
With His Words I Did Agree.
So I Bought A Bunch Of Every Colour,
To Remember What He Told Me.

IN A DREAM

In A Dream The Good Lord Told Me,
He Would Give Me Kingdoms Made Out Of Gold.
If I Wanted Much More Than This,
I Could Have Riches And Wealth Untold.
Famous He Would Make Me,
Or Could I Be A Queen.
God Just Smiled When I Told Him,
The Best Thing I Have Seen.
Are My Children Laughing,
Their Faces Aglow With Glee.
Just To See Them Every Morning,
All As Happy As Can Be.
I Do Not Want Fame Or Power,
I Do Not Need Your Riches Untold.
My Family Is My Treasure,
Worth More To Me Than Gold.

MY ANGEL

I Sat On A Park Bench One Day,
As I Watched The World Go By.
I Tried To Think Of Happier Times,
All I Could Do Was Cry.
I Hoped That You Were Happy,
That I Would See You Again.
I Wondered How My Heart Still Beat,
When It Carried So Much Pain.
Just When I Thought My Heart Would Break,
A Mist Came Down On Me.
At First I Could See Nothing,
Then A Bright Light I Could See.
It Was Then I Saw You Clearly,
It Felt Just Like A Dream.
I Saw You In Heavens Garden,
Standing By A Sparkling Stream.
Your Face Was Aglow With Sunshine,
It Was Such A Lovely Sight.
Like The Sun That Shone Around You,
Bathed In God's Heavenly Light.
Angels Were Gathered Around You,
With Love Ones Who Had Gone Before.
You Looked So Well And Happy,
I Could Not Have Asked For More.
You Glimpsed Me For A Moment,
I Thought I Saw You Wave.
As The Mist Was Fading,
I Saw The Smile You Gave.
God Showed Me You Are In Heaven,
An Angel You Surely Must Be.

For When You Lived Upon This Earth,
You Were A Beautiful Angel To Me.

THE VISIT

One Night While I Was Sleeping,
I Heard A Song So Sweet.
I Awoke And Saw An Angel,
Standing At My Feet.
She Told Me Not To Be Afraid,
You Are Lucky Do You Not See.
Your Prayers The Lord Has Answered,
There Is A Place You Would Like To Be.,
She Put Her Had In My Hand,
Said Please Come With Me.
Very Few Go On This Journey,
To See What You Will See.
We Flew Over Emerald Mountains,
Past A Deep Blue Sea.
It Was When I Saw My Dear Mother,
I Knew Where I Must Be..
Her Garden Was So Beautiful,.
The Trees And Flowers So Bright.
Where She Was Felt Wonderful,.
Bathed In God's Heavenly Light.
She Is Living With The Angels Now,
Free From All Toil And Pain.
Though She Misses Her Family,
She Would Not Come Back Again.
I Held Her For A Moment,
They Said I Had To Go.
I Kissed Her On Her Dear Sweet Face,
I Told Her I Loved Her So.
Then I Woke Up In My Bedroom,
In The Dark Was One Bright Beam..

Did I Really Visit Heaven,
Or Was It All A Dream.

ANGELS

Have You Ever Seen An Angel,
Have You Ever Felt Its Glow.
For Angels Stand Beside Us,
More Often Than We Know.
When You Carry Heavy Burdens,
When Your Heart Is Sore With Grief.
Your Angels Take Your Worries,
To Give You Some Relief.
Sometimes Your Soul Is Troubled,
Your Life Too Hard To Bear.
God Will Never Leave You Lonely,
Your Angels Are Always There.

I PEEKED IN HEAVEN'S GATE

I Was Walking One Morning,
I Was Crying In The Rain.
How Could I Go On Living,
With My Heart In So Much Pain.
When I Turned The Corner,
I Heard A Laugh I Knew.
Then I Felt A Mist Surround Me,
It Was Then I First Saw You.
You Were In A Beautiful Garden,
With Bright Flowers All Around.
The Angels Were All Singing,
It Was The Sweetest Sound.
I Saw My Mother And Father,
With Loved Ones Who Had Gone Before.
They All Looked So Well And Happy,
I Could Not Have Asked For More.
I Wandered Off The Pathway,
Then I Peeked In Through The Gate.
I Knew I Was Too Early,
That I Would Have To Wait.
Then It Started Fading,
The Scene Just Went From View.
My Heart Had Stopped Its Aching,
It Had Stopped Raining Too.
I Often Walk Along That Road,
But Can Not Find You Again.
God Let Me Peek In Heavens Garden,
To Take Away My Pain.

PHONE HEAVEN

I Wish I Could Phone Heaven,
To Have A Nice Long Chat With You,
To See What You Are Doing,
Ask How You Are Feeling Too.
I Miss The Talks We Used To Have,
For Hours, How Did Time Fly.
Then The Shock I Got That Day,
You Had Gone Without Saying Goodbye.
I Often Hear A Voice Like Yours,
Or Meet Someone With The Same Spark.
In Their Eyes, My Heart Lights Up With,
Gladness, Only Then I Realise.
That I Will Not See You Again,
At Least Not Here On Earth.
Someone Who Loved Me My Whole Life.
Who Cared For Me From Birth.
No Sister To Sit And Talk To,
To Tell All My Joys And Fears.
But You Left Me Beautiful Memories,
Of All Those Special Years.

MY SOUL MATE

There Is A Man I Love So Much,
He Lives At My Address.
He Gives Me Everything I Need,
Plus Lots Of Happiness.
His Family Mean The World To Him,
I Know Our Children Are His Life.
He Has Kept All His Promises,
Since He Made Me His Wife.
Life Sometimes Has Its Problems,
He Always Gets Us Through.
Just As Long As We Are Happy,
He Will Be Content Too.
I Hope That Life Is Good To Us,
We Can Stay Together Until We Grow Old.
Then We Can See Our Children Grow Up,
And Watch All Their Dreams Unfold.
Now That I Have My Children,
With The Love Of My Life Too.
All My Loving Friends And Family,
My Dreams Have All Come True.
I Could Not Find Another Man Like Him,
If I Searched High And Low,
Maybe If I Asked His Mother,
I Bet That She Would Know.
I Can Not Tell Him To His Face,
That Is Why I Wrote This Verse.
But I Might Shout It From The Rooftops,
That I Am The Luckiest Women On Earth.

I GLIMPSED HEAVEN

I Saw Myself Walking,
Across A Sparkling Stream.
When I Saw The Beauty,
I Thought It Was A Dream.
The Flowers Were So Beautiful,
They Were Dancing In The Breeze.
I Heard The Birds All Singing,
Amongst The Apple Trees.
When I Saw You Standing,
Beside A Sea Of Blue.
As You Turned And Looked My Way,
It Was Then I New.
That You Had Gone To Heaven,
Then I Saw You Wave,
I Knew That You Were Happy,
Just By The Smile You Gave.
Then It Started Fading,
A Mist Came Over Me.
But I Know I Went To Heaven,
Where I Glimpsed Eternity.

THE QUESTION

I Asked The Lord A Question,
Why Did She Have To Go.
My Mother Was My Best Friend,
And I Loved Her So.
The Lord He Did Not Answer,
So I Asked Again.
Then He Softly Told Me,
I Took Away Her Pain.
Now She Lives With Me In Heaven,
A Honour That Was Her Due.
I Know That You Love Her,
But I Love Her Too.
She Has Not Gone Forever,
She Is With You Night And Day.
Although You Can Not See Her,
She Is Never Far Away.
So Do Not Be Heartbroken,
Please Do Not Be Sad.
She Has Gone On To Paradise,
Waiting With Your Dad.

THAT SPECIAL SOMEONE

Do You Have That Special Someone,
That You Can Depend Upon.
Some People Search A Life Time,
They Never Find That Special One.
Someone You Would Give Your Life For,
They Would Do The Same For You.
As Long As You Were Happy,
They Would Be Happy Too.
Where Do You Find A Love Like That?
Some Folk Just Want To Know.
With Love You Have To Nourish It,
Then You Will See It Grow.
At First It Starts As A Spark,
Then Soon Becomes A Flame.
Stay Together Through Thick And Thin,
Plus All The Joy And Pain.
Then This Love Should Last A Life Time,
The Reason That I Know.
I Found The Love Of My Life,
Over Forty Years Ago.

FLOWERS FOR ANGELS

Why Do Angels All Love Flowers,
I Cannot Remember Who Told Me.
When You Walk Into A Garden,
Can You Feel The Harmony.
See The Flowers And Watch Them Sparkle,
Like The Colours Of Angels Wings.
If You Sit And Wait A Moment,
The Angels They Might Tell You Things.
When You Stop And Quietly Listen,
You Might Hear An Angel Sing.
Maybe Feel A Glow Around You,
Then A Message They May Bring.
So Think Of This When You See Flowers,
Think Of Angels And The Songs They Sing.
The Message That They Always Bring You,
Is God Loves Every Living Thing.

MY LOVE

My Love How Much I Miss You,
Now That You Are Gone.
I Feel My Life Is Empty,
I Can Not Carry On.
My Days Are Dark And Gloomy,
My Nights Are Lonely Too.
Even When I Am Sleeping,.
My Dreams Are All Of You.
Friends Say That Time Will Heal Me,
They Say My Heart Will Mend.
I Have Loved You For A Lifetime,
My Lover And My Best Friend.
Our Hearts Once Beat Together,
Now My Heart Beats Alone.
A Part Of Me Is Missing,
Now That I Am On My Own.
I Hope I Will Meet You In Heaven,
Until Then Please Be My Guide.
I Will Hold You In My Arms Again,
Never To Leave Your Side.

NEVER BUY

What Can Money Never Buy,
Can It Buy A Smile.
Can It Buy A Cheerful Word,
To Make Your Life Worthwhile.
Can It Buy A Pair Of Eyes,
Or Calm A Troubled Soul.
When Your Heart Is Broken,
Can It Make It Whole.
What About The Love You Get,
Or The Love You Give.
Can It Buy You Happiness,
Or Buy The Will To Live.
Can It Buy The Gentle Breeze,
Or The Sun And Rain.
Can It Buy Some Tender Care,
To Make You Well Again.
Can It Buy The Love Of God,
And Make All Your Dreams Come True.
Love And Faith, Joy Good Health,
Costs Nothing, But It Is Up To You.

CONTENTMENT

The Old Year Is Now Ended,
A New Year Has Begun.
We Must Decide What Path To Take,
Should We Slowly Walk Or Run.
Shall We Take Things Easy,
Or Eagerly Press Ahead.
Do We Try To Fulfil Our Dreams,
Or Be Content To Stay In Bed.
If You Had A New Years Wish,
That God Could Make Come True.
Would You Waste It On Silly Dreams,
And Selfish Things For You,
Ask God For Contentment,
Not For Power Or Greed.
If God Did Grant You This One Wish,
You Would Have Everything You Need.
Just Think, To Always Be Content,
No Matter What Comes Your Way.
Even In Our Worst Times,
There Is Always A Better Day.
With Contentment There Comes Peace,
You Can Believe You Will Reach Your Goal..
Instead Of Feeling Half Alive,
Your Spirit Now Feels Whole.
God Can Make You Feel Like This,
This Contentment He Can Give.
Trust In Him With All Your Heart,
Then You Will Start To Live.
So Welcome In This New Year,
Say That You Are Glad It Is Here.

Knowing That God Loves You,
Every Year Will Hold No Fear.
So I Wish You All The Best,
With Joy And Good Health Too.
Most Of All I Wish Contentment.
That Will Last Your Whole Life Through.

IF YOU NEED A FRIEND

If You Are Feeling Sad And Lonely,
Sometimes You Need A Friend.
If Your Dreams Are All Broken,
And All Your Heartaches Will Not Mend.
Go On Your Knees And Call Him,
The Lord He Will Come To You.
If You Ask Him He Will Be There,
Your Best Friend So Good And True.
You Will See The Sun Will Come Out,
All Your Hopes Will Soon Appear.
Call His Name,don't Let Your Heart Doubt,
Ask Him, And He Will Soon Be Here.

A BROKEN HEART

When Friends Say Do You Still Miss Him,
Just How Can I Explain.
I Miss Him Like The Sparkling Streams,
That Run Dry Without The Rain.
I Miss Him Like The Forests Would,
If They Cut Down All The Trees.
Just As Much As Flowers,
If There Were No Birds And Bees.
Sometimes I Want To Tell Them,
I Would Just Like To Say.
I Miss Him More Than Life Itself,
Every Single Day.
He Was My Lifetime Partner,
We Had Never Been Apart.
He Was My First And Last Love,
Who I Loved With All My Heart.
I Know He Is With The Angels Now,
At Peace And Free From Pain.
Though I Miss Him So Much,
I Do Not Wish Him Back To Suffer Again.
I Can Not Tell My Friends All This,
If They Ask I Just Say I Am Fine.
They Always Smile And Answer,
You Will Heal Just Give It Time.
I Know They Are Only Being Kind,
Though At Times The Teardrops Start.
I Think If They Ask Me Again,
I Will Say Ask My Broken Heart.

A LETTER FROM HEAVEN

To My Dear Daughter,
I Am Writing You This Letter,from Heaven Up
   Above.
In It I Want To Send You, All My Thanks And Love.
I Want You To Know I Am Happy,
So Glad To Be Free From Pain.
Even Though I Miss You All,i Would Not Come
   Back Again.
I Want You To Be Happy, To You
My Prayers I Have Sent.live A Life That Is
Full Of Joy, And Try To Be Content.
You Have Not Got A Million Years Left On
This Earth,so Get All Your Living Done.
Do Your Very Best My Daughter, Live Your
Life Always In The Sun.
You Know I Was Tired And Weary,
The Lord He Knew It Too.
He Sent His Angels For Me,and In Their Arms
I Quickly Flew. They Took Me Straight To Heaven,
To Meet Those Who Had Gone Before.
So My Dear Do Not Wish Me Back Again,
To Suffer Anymore.
I Know That You Still Grieve For Me,
When You Weep It Makes Me Sad.
I Just Want You To Remember, All The Good
Years That I Had, Can You Not Tell That I
Am Happy, The Clock Of Life Is Set.
So Dry Your Eyes And Think Of The Laughter,
The Bad Times Just Forget.
I Will Always Be With You My Dear Daughter,

The Rest Of My Family Too.
I Am Living With The Angels In Paradise,
Just Waiting For All Of You.
      Love From Your Mother XXX.

GIFTS

When On Our Knees We Pray To God,
For Gifts Both Great And Small.,
Dear Friends Why Not Ask Him For,
The Greatest Gifts Of All..
Ask Him To Fill Your Heart With Love,
Or Give You A Peaceful Soul..
For You To Have The Healing Touch,
To Make Sore Bodies Whole.
Ask Him To Give You Kindness,
To Give You A Caring Mind.
I Know That If You Had These Things,
I Am Sure That That You Will Find.
These Are Treasures Worth
Much More Than Gold,
A Rich Man You Would Be,
To Think These Things That Are
Worth So Much, The Lord Has Give You Free.
So Are You Going To Ask Him,
For Gifts Both Great And Small.
Or Will You Ask For Gods Love,
The Greatest Gift Of All..

TRUE LOVE

Have You Always Wanted True Love,
Looked A Lifetime With No Success.
Where Is This Thing They Are Seeking,
Love Always Comes With Happiness.
I Know Some Folk Who Try And Buy It,
We All Know That Love Is Free.
You Can Give It Or Receive It,
Where It Is God Will Always Be.
God Can Give This Love You Are Seeking,
If You Are Asking Him He Will Bring.
All The Love Your Heart Has Longed For,
He Will Make Your Spirit Sing.
The Love He Gives Is So Special,
Hope And Joy Will Flood Your Soul..
Your Poor Heart That Felt So Empty,
If It Is Broken,god Can Make It Whole.
Tell Your Friends Tell Everybody,
About The Love That God Can Bring.
Shout This Message To The Whole World,
That God Loves Every Living Thing.

ONE WISH

If You Could Have One Wish,
I Wonder What It Would Be,
Will You Ask For Fame Or Power,
Perhaps Be A Celebrity.
Maybe Have A Brain Like Einstein,
Have Knowledge By The Score.
Just Enough Money To Live On,
But Maybe You Want More.
I Know What I Would Ask For,
If One Wish I Was Sent.
Health And Love For All My Family,
With That I Would Be Content.

MAYBE

Do You See The Lonely People,
Do You Not Really Care.
Maybe You Walk Past Them,
You Do Not Realise They Are There.
If You Only Gave Them Just A Smile,
Or A Simple Word Or Two.
You Will Feel That You Have Done Your Bit,
Maybe Cheer Yourself Up Too.
These Few Words Might Become A Chat,
That You Do Not Want To End.
You Never Know A Simple Smile,
Could Get You A New Best Friend.

THE ANSWER

Love And Kindness Is The Answer,
I Just Hope That You Agree.
War And Killing Is Not Wanted,
Why Not Love Your Enemy.
Once My Heart Was Filled With Darkness,
I Simply Did Not Care.
I Thought That God Had Left Me,
Then I Found Him Waiting There.
Now He Fills My Heart With Sunshine,
Fills My Soul With Light And Love.
I Know He Will Always Be There,
As He Guides Me From Above.
The Lord Will Not Desert You,
If You Ask And Show You Care.
He Will Always Stay Beside You,
And Be With You Everywhere.
Many Times I Have Forgot Him,
Lot's Of Times I Tried To Flee.
God I Know, Will Never Leave Me,
For When I Run, He Runs With Me.
If You Want This Peace He Gives You,
Ask Him, And He Will Enter In.
Knock On His Door, Until He Answers,
Do Not Let The Devil Win.

MIRACLES

Some People Ask For Miracles,
While Others Do Not Believe.
There Is A Miracle In The Sunshine,
In All The Air We Breathe.
There Are Miracles In The Countryside,
If We Just Rest Awhile.
A Miracle In The Rain That Falls,
And In A Baby's Smile.
The Best Miracle Of All, Is The Love
That We Feel For Others,
This World Would Be Like Paradise,
If We Loved Everyone As Brothers.
This World Needs Our Prayers,
It Needs Our Love,
For The Plants And Animals Too.
Give Love To Every Living Thing,
The Same Way God Loves You.

FRIENDSHIP

Ask Your Angels To Surround You,
When Your Pain Will Never End.
They Will Love You And Protect You,
All Your Heartaches They Will Mend.
They Will Help You Through Your Troubles,
Until On Your Feet You Firmly Stand.
Never Be Afraid To Ask Them,
They Will Hold You By The Hand.
You May Doubt What I Have Told You,
God Has Said Our Will Is Free.
What Harm Is There In Asking,
Look What God Has Done For Me.

IN LOVE MANY TIMES

You Can Have Many Loves In A Lifetime,
That Is What Some Folk Say.
They Say That Love Can Last For Years,
Or Maybe Just A Day.
It Might Be A Fleeting Moment,
Or Last Till The End Of Time.
You Can Compare It To A Fizzy Drink,
Or Perhaps A Sparkling Wine.
This True Love That You Read About,
Do You Think It Is Easy To Find?
Where One Can Not Live Without The Other,
Their Two Hearts Are Forever Entwined.
That Special Someone Who Loves You,
More Than Life, Without You They Not Whole.
You Would Gladly Give Them Your Last Breath,
Their Happiness Is Your Goal..
So Do You Want Someone Special?
Well Maybe You And Me,
Can Strike A Spark, And Make A Flame,
That Will Last For Eternity.

LIFES COMPANION

You Have Lost Your Lifes Companion,
A Life Linked To Your Own.
Sometimes You Think You Are Dreaming,
That You Are Now Alone.
He Has Crossed Over The Bridge Of Love,
To Meet Loved Ones, On The Other Side.
Now His Toil And Pain Is Over,
His Love Can Still Be Your Guide.
He Will Comfort You In Bad Times,
Then He Will Hold You When You Weep.
When You Doubt He Will Give You Faith,
He Will Soothe You When You Sleep.
I Am Sure That He Will Tell You,
At Night Time In Your Dreams.
That He Will Always Be There,
No Matter How Hard It Seems.
If You Listen You May Hear Him Whisper,
We Have A Bond That Nothing Can Sever.
I Once Made You A Promise My Love,
That I Would Stay With You Forever.

FREE WILL

When You Are Feeling Sad And Lonely,
Or Feeling In Dispair.
Ask The Dear Lord To Help You,
His Angels Will Soon Be There.
Never Think That You Are Not Worthy,
For God Loves Everyone The Same.
If You Want Him To Help You,
You Just Have To Call Out His Name.
God Gave To Us All Free Will.,
If You Wish You Can Stay On Your Own.
God Will Always Be Waiting,
If You Do Not Want To Struggle Alone.
Be Not Afraid To Ask Him,
He Will Heal Your Body And Soul..
His Angels Will Gently Enfold You,
They Will Comfort And Make You Whole.
You Are Never Alone In This Lifetime,
Your Angels Are There From Your Birth.
They Want To Love And Guide You,
On Lifes Journey Here On Earth.
God Doe's Not Care If You Are Famous,
It Will Not Matter If You Are Rich Or Poor.
If Your Heart Has Love And Kindness ,
God Will Stay With You For Sure.
So Dear Friends Just Call Him,
If You Need A Shoulder To Lean Upon.
He Will Give You The Strength To Recover,
Then All Of Your Doubts Will Be Gone.
Just Think Of The Peace God Can Give You,
Easing Your Hurt And Your Pain.

Knowing That Gods Always With You,
To Never Be Lonely Again.

GOD'S FLOWER

God Came Down To Earth's Garden,
He Looked Around Awhile.
Then He Saw Your Weary Body,
He Saw Your Lovely Smile.
He Knew That You Were Tired,
A Cure Was Not To Be.
So He Wrapped His Arms Around You,
And He Whispered Come With Me.
Your Pain And Trials Are Over,
I Know You Have Done Your Best.
Your Life On Earth Is Ended Now,
I Am Going To Take You Home To Rest.
You Will Miss Your Loved Ones,
And They Will Miss You Too.
But One Day In My Heaven,
They Will Meet Up Again With You.
So Go Now With My Angels,
See Loved Ones Who Have Gone Before.
I Am Taking You To Paradise,
To Live With Me For Evermore.

MY FATHER

My Father He Really Loved Me,
Just How Much Can Never Be Told,
When God First Made My Father,
He Must Of Broke The Mould.
I Can Not Find A Man More Faithful,
A Man So Kind And Good.
Though I Tried My Hardest,
I Knew I Never Would.
It Is Years Now Since I Lost Him,
It Feels Like Only Yesterday.
I Still Can Feel His Presence,
He Has Never Gone Away.
His Hand Is Always On My Shoulder,
He Guides Me Night And Day.
When I Am Needing Comfort,
He Is Never Far Away.
One Day We Will Be Together,
At Some Future Date,
He Will Be With My Dear Mother,
Waiting At Heavens Gate.

DO YOU BELIEVE

So You Think There Is No Heaven,
Or Believe In Angels Too.
If You Want Me To Prove It,
I Will Tell You Want To Do.
Ask The Lord To Send Some Angels,
If You Ask They Will Appear.
Close Your Eyes, And You Will Feel Them,
You Will Know When They Draw Near.
A Warmth Will Then Enfold You,
With The Comfort An Angel Brings.
You Will Feel A Glow Around You,
Reflecting From Their Sparkling Wings.
You Will Know Them By Their Beauty,
A Message Of Joy And Hope They Bring.
If You Doubt After All I Have Told You,
You Will Never Believe In Anything.
In Time You May Come To Realise,
With The Sorrows And Joys Life Brings.
You Might Open Your Eyes And See Them,
The Angels With Their Sparkling Wings.

LIFE'S PARTNER

Sitting Alone In My Garden,
My Thoughts Were All With You.
I Had A Picture In My Mind,
Of All We Used To Do.
I Remember The Day I Met You,
And The Special Date When We Were Wed.
I Promise To Never Leave You,
You So Often Said.
You Had To Break Your Promise,
For The Years Had Took Their Toil.
Now I Feel Just Half Alive,
You Were My Heart And Soul.
How Quickly Life And Time Has Gone,
The Years Did Simply Fly.
Just At The Best Time Of Our Life,
We Had To Say Goodbye.
Most Times We Laughed, Sometimes We Cried,
We Thought We Would Live Forever.
Our Lives Were Filled With Love And Smiles,
We Danced Through Life Together.
But My Partner Is Now Gone,
My Dancing Days Are Over.
No One To Share My Life With,
No More Leaning On Your Shoulder.
When I Take That Pathway,
On The Journey We All Must Make.
You Will Be There To Guide Me,
In Every Step I Take.
I Will Fold My Arms Around You,
You Will Do The Same.

We Will Be Together In Heavens Garden,
When The Lord Calls Out My Name.

ASK HIM

If The World Looks Dark And Gloomy,
And Your Life Looks Bleak And Bare.
Ask The Lord To Give You Comfort,
He Will Send A Angel There.
If Your Heart Feels Tired And Heavy,
You Think You Might Give In.
Pray For Love And Guidance,
With God I Know You Will Win.
Close Youe Eyes, Ask Him To Help You.
Say Lord I Need You Here?
He Will Wrap His Arms Around You,
Then He Will Banish Every Tear.
Why Not Ask God To Help You,
If You Do He Will Give You Peace.
The Lord Will Not Forsake You,
His Love And Comfort Will Never Cease.

YOU WALK WITH ME

I Now Walk This Life Alone,
Where Once You Walked With Me.
I Feel A Space Inside My Heart,
A Gap Where You Used To Be.
I Feel A Coldness Here Inside,
It Is Deep Within My Soul.
Now My Heart Is Half Alive,
With You It Once Was Whole.
I Remember How Much I Loved You,
I Hope And Pray You Knew.
That You Were The World To Me,
You Made My Dreams Come True.
Our Family Is Grown And Happy Now,
For That I Should Be Glad,
But There Is A Longing In My Heart,
For You And The Life We Had.
So I Will Travel Along Life's Pathway,
Be It Happy Times Or Sad.
I Will Think About The Good Times,
Plus The Many Happy Years We Had.
I Know I Will Not Be Lonely,
For Now I Can Truly See.
That Every Road That I Walk Along,
You Will Walk That Path With Me.

MY CHILD

If All The World Were Mine To Give,
I Would Give It All To You.
Bestow You Every Happiness,
To Last Your Whole Life Through.
I Would Help You Climb Life's Mountains,
Try And Banish Every Pain..
Every Single Day, I Would Give You,
Summer, Without The Rain..
Alas These Things I Cannot Grant You,
My Child It Is Up To You.
Love And Care Is What You Need Most,
Plus My Prayers To Help You Through.
I Wish Joy To You My Dear One,
May All Your Dreams Come True.
Give Love To Every Living Thing,
I Will Be Always There For You.

SILVER LINING'S

All Clouds Have Silver Lining's,
That Is What Some People Say.
The Sun Will Start To Shine Again,
Now All My Skies Are Grey.
Some Folk Can Here The Birds Sing,
They Are As Happy As Can Be.
So Why Am I So Gloomy,
What Is Wrong With Me.
If God Would Just Give Me A Sign,
To Show That You Are Near.
If I Could Glimpse You For A Moment,
It Might Take Away This Fear.
I Feel That You Have Left Me,
That I Will Never See You Again.
Dear Lord, Answer Me This Prayer,
Take Away This Bitter Pain.
That Night As I Lay Sleeping,
I Seemed To Hear My Loved One Say
I Am Here With You My Love,
I Have Not Gone Away.
You Know I Have Will Never Leave You,
His Voice So Softly Said,
I Awoke And He Was Smiling,
Standing At My Bed.
He Said That He Was So Happy,
That I Had A Lot More Work To Do.
If I Put My Faith In God,
He Would Help Me To Get Through.
Dawn Broke Just As I Woke Up,
I Heard A Blackbird Sing.

I Felt That My Dull Winter,
Had Just Turned Into Spring.
My Love Gave Me A Promise,
Though Him I Cannot See.
That I Never Will Be Lonely,
He Is Always There With Me.

I NEED YOU

Do You Know How Much I Miss You,
I Think My Heart Will Break.
I Toss And Turn When Sleeping,
I Weep When I Am Awake.
How Do You Go On Living,
When Half Of You Is Gone,
My Heart Thinks You Are With Me,
It Still Beats For Two Not One.
They Have Always Beat Together,
A Lifetime Seems A Lot.
Friends Tell Me I Was Lucky,
To Have Had The Years We Got.
So I Will Try To Keep On Walking,
Along This Path We All Must Plod,
I Will Bless The Years I Had With You,
And Leave The Rest To God.

FINDING GOD

You Will Find God In A Garden,
I Heard Somebody Say.
I Have Looked For Him For Years Now,
I Search Most Every Day.
I Can Never Find Him,
He Tries To Hide From Me,
They Say If God Is With You,
So Happy You Will Be.
He Will Help With All Your Worries,
Plus He Can Bring You Peace.
You Never Will Be Lonely,
Gods Love Will Never Cease.
So When I Awoke One Morning,
I Asked God If He Was There,
I Seemed To Here Him Answer,
My Child, I Am Everywhere.
To Find Him You Must Ask Him,
You Will Never Have Regret,
If I Had Not Called To Him That Morning,
I Would Still Be Searching Yet.
God Is There In A Garden,
I Knew This From The Start,
The Best Place You Will Find Him.
Is Deep Within Your Heart.

A CANDLE

Life Is Like A Candle,
Flames Go High And Low.
Sometimes In Our Bad Times,
We Have No Place To Go.
Once This Happened To Me,
My Heart Was Racked With Pain.
Instead Of Life's Bright Sunshine,
I Just Had Clouds And Rain.
Then I Asked The Lord This Question,
Dear God, Are You There?
I Soon Received His Answer,
Yes I Am Everywhere!
Clouds Often Surround Me,
I Am Not Perfect I Still Sin.
When Life Gets Too Much For Me,
I Simply Ask Him In.

TWO SPECIAL PEOPLE

There Are Two Special People,
Who My Heart Can Not Forget.
The Way That They Cared For Me,
Is Locked In My Memory Yet.
Their Family Were The World To Them,
Our Childhood Was Fun And Play.
They Gave Us Everything They Could,
And Loved Us Come What May.
My Father Went To Heaven First,
Hard Work Had Took Its Toil.
He Had Done His Duty Well,
Raising Us Was His Last Goal.
My Dear Mother Joined Him Later,
I Still Remember, What She Told Me.
I Love You So My Daughter,
But With Your Father I Want To Be.
I Am Tired Of All This Suffering,
God Knows I Have Done My Best.
My Body Is Sore And Weary,
My Tired Soul Is In Need Of Some Rest.
I Did My Best To Comfort Her,
And Tried To Ease Her Pain.
Too Soon Her Time Had Come Around,
I Lost My Angel, That Heaven Would Gain.
I Hope They Are Together Now,
Just As Happy As They Were Before.
My Mother In Gods Beautiful Garden,
With My Dear Father Forever More.
Even Though I Know I Have Lost Them,
I Do Not Feel That They Are Gone,

And In My Weakest Moments,
I Feel Them Urge Me On.
It Is Only Now That I Realise,
That Love Can Never Die,
Our Loved Ones Are All Around Us,
Not Just Somewhere In The Sky.
I Often Walk Down Memory Lane,
Back To Them, And The Love That We Had.
I Just Want To Say With All My Heart,
Thank You, My Dear Mam And Dad.

FOR A DEAR FRIEND

One Day The Sun Will Come Out,
The Clouds Will Fade From View.
Then Your Heart Will Sing Again,
This My Friend Is Up To You.
God Tells Us That We Have Free Will,
We Decide Ourselves Our Fate.
Your Life Could Be So Wonderful,
You Can Do It So Why Wait.
Trust The Lord He Can Help You,
He Will Ease Your Heartache Too,
You Have So Much To Live For,
There Are So Many Things To Do.
Do You Think Of Those Who Have No Food,
The Homeless And The Blind,
They Wish They Had A Life Like Yours,
If You Think Of This You Will Find,
A Peace Will Come Over You,
Contentment Will Set In,
Never Think That You Will Lose,
Always Think That You Will Win.
So My Dear Friend, Please Do Your Best,
Ask Help From God Above,
You Possess The Most Precious Thing,
You Have Your Familie's Love.

WHITE ROSE'S

When I Buy White Rose's, What Do I See,
I Can Picture A Face Of A Angel,
That Is What You Were To Me.
You Had A Smile So Gentle,
A Face That Was So Fair.
Sometimes I Think I Am Dreaming,
When I Look And Your Not There.
I Know That We Were So Lucky,
To Have The Years We Had,
I Have Tried To Take The Good Times,
Along With All The Bad.
I Know You Are In Heaven,
That You Have Passed Lifes Test,
I Often Hear Folk Saying,
God Always Takes The Best.
These Flowers That Were
Your Favourites,
In A Vase I Place With Care.
As I Slowly Light A Candle,
I Feel That You Are There.

SEEKING

Have You Found What You Are Looking For,
Do You Search In Vain.
Some Folk Look For Selfish Things,
And Just Live Their Lives For Gain.
They Go Searching In The Forests,
Dive To The Bottom Of The Sea,
Everybody Is Looking For Something,
So What Can That Something Be.
Are They Seeking Buried Treasure,
Digging In Deep Mines For Gold,
Can They Be Seeking Knowledge,
Or Searching For Secrets Of Old.
Maybe I Should Tell Them,
It Is Easy As Can Be.
Just Ask God To Find Them,
The Same Way That He Found Me.
Then You Will Have What You Have
Been Looking For,
A Joy Will Come To You,
He Will Keep You Safe Forever,
With A Love So Strong And True.
Pray To God And You Will Find Him,
You Will Never Have A Better Friend,
At Last, You Will Find What You Have Been
    Seeking,
On That Day All Your Searching Will End.

MY HEART

Friends Say I Will Find A New Love,
My Poor Heart Will Not Agree.
It Thinks You Might Come Back Again,
To Be The Way It Used To Be.
It Skips A Beat When It Hears Your Name,
Or A Face Like Yours I See.
I Can Tell That My Heart Is Still Missing You,
By The Ache I Feel In Me.
Friends Say That I Must Forget You,
I Tell Them I Have Tried.
That I No Longer Love You,
But My Heart Knows I Have Lied.
I Hope One Day I Will Meet Someone,
A New Love To End This Pain.
On That Day My Poor Heart Will Be Mended,
Then It Won't Want You Back Again..

JUST GO FOR IT

Do You Stay In Bed On A Morning,
Or Do You Get Up And Go.
Are You Finding Life A Hard Struggle,
Maybe You Just Go With The Flow.
Is Your Heart As Light As A Feather,
Nothing Much Gets You Down.
Is There A Smile On Your Face,
Or More Usually Just A Frown.
Do You Know That God Loves You.
Have You Got Faith In Your Soul..
Your Heart Feels Half Alive,
But You Wish You Could Make It Whole.
Take A Chance, Just Go For It,
Try And Reach For The Moon.
You Can Lose Nothing By Trying,
For Time Runs Out Far Too Soon.
If You Get To The Moon.
Then Reach For The Stars
Try And Make Your Dreams Come True.
When Life Gets Too Much Of A Burdon,
Ask The Lord To Help You Through,
He Will Guide You In Your Weak Times,
He Will Ease You Past Your Pain.
You Will Have Something To Live For,
He Will Make You Well Again,
Do You Want To Be Like Your Neighbour,
Who Is Full To The Brim With Love,
Maybe They Believe In The Dear Lord,
And A Heaven Up Above.
So Ask The Lord To Help You,

Rise And Shine When You Awake
Live For Every Moment,
Eagerly Wait For Each Dawn To Break
My Friend It Is So Easy To Do,
You Can Achieve This Don't You See.
The Way That You Are Feeling Now,
Is Just How I Used To Be..

SAFE IN MY HEART

When I Am Sitting On My Own,
My Thoughts Go Back To You.
To The Times We Spent Together,
With A Love So Warm And True.
You Often Said If I Went First,
That It Would Break Your Heart.
Now It Is My Heart That Is Broken.
Since We Have Been Apart.
Even When I Go Out Walking,
My Eye's Still Look For You.
If You Were Around The Corner,
Then My Prayers Would All Come True .
Often I Meet Someone,
Who Has The Same Sparkle In Their Eye's,
My Heart Lights Up With Gladness,
Only Then I Realise.
That You Are Now In Heaven,
The Lord Has Eased Your Pain.
My Heart Is Always Yearning,
To Have You Home Again.
For Me There Is No Sunny Weather,
My Skies Are All Stormy And Grey.
I Only Know Without You,
There Is No Perfect Day.
But I Still Have My Beautiful Memories,
They Are Locked Safe In My Heart.
Treasures No One Can Steal From Me,
From Which I Will Never Part.
In My Dreams I Hear You Whisper,
That You Are With Me Still,

You Say That You Will Not Leave Me,
And Promise You Never Will.
Years Ago You Made A Vow To Me,
That We Would Never Part.
And You Have Kept Your Promise,
You Are There Inside My Heart.

LET HIM IN

At Times Your Soul Is Weary,
Your Heart Feels Tired And Sore.
You Think You Have No Reason,
To Go On Living Anymore.
Ask The Lord Above To Help You,
Keep On Trying, Do Not Give In.
He Will Bring You What You Need Most.
If You Only Ask Him In.
He Will Soothe Away Your Troubles,
Then Ease Your Every Pain.
He Will Grant You Peace Forever.
You Will Never Doubt Again.
His Angels Will Surround You,
Why Suffer,can't You See?
They Will Love You And Protect You,
And Will Set You Spirit Free.
Ask The Lord To Be There,
If You Do Not Ask,then He Won't Come In.
Knock On His Door, And He Will Answer.
God Will Show You How To Win.
Do You Know How Much God Loves You,
The Lord Love's Everyone The Same.
If You Turn Your Back, He Will Not Enter,
Do It Now, Call His Name.

WHY

I Think I Must Be Dreaming,
I Cannot Believe Its True.
Why Is This World Still Turning,
Doe's It Know, That I Lost You.
Why Are People So Cheerful,
They Are Even Laughing In The Rain.
For Me There Are No Silver Lining's,
No Rainbows To Come After Rain.
The Dreams We Planned Together,
Now I Must Do On My Own.
I See Couples Holding Each Other,
But I Am Always Alone.
My Eyes Are Red From Weeping,
Since My Love Has Gone.
I Am Feeling Guilty,you Would
Want Me To Journey On.
So Stay Close To Me My Dear One.
Guide Me On Life's Road Past This Pain.
Help Me Climb The Mountains Of Sorrow,
Until I Stand On Lifes Peek Once Again.

CALL TO HEAVEN

I Cannot Find The Words To Tell You,
I Do Not Know What To Say.
But I Should Have Told You This,
Before You Went Away.
Now My Heart Is Broken,
I Cannot End This Bitter Pain.
If Only I Could Have You Back,
So I Would Have The Chance Again.
To Tell You How Much You Mean To Me,
That I Loved You So.
The Reason I Did Not Tell You Then,
I Thought That You Would Know.
That You Were Everything To Me.
You Made My Dreams Come True.
So I Am Sending A Message To Heaven,
That I Will Never Stop Loving You.

FRIEND'S

Have You Friends, Who Are Kind And Caring,
When You Need Them, They Are There.
Your Dreams And Doubts They Are Sharing,
In Good And Bad Times They Still Care.
They Know Your Faults ,but They Still Love You.
Give Good Advice To See You Through.
You Know They Will Never Hurt You,
Loyal Friends So Good And True.
If You Can Keep Them For A Lifetime,
Stay Good Friends Until You Grow Old.
You Will Not Need Wealth, Or Lots Of Treasures,
What You Have Is Worth More Than Gold.

GOD'S ROSE

I Asked God If You Were Happy,
To Let Me Feel You Near.
In My Dreams That Night,
God Came To Me, He Whispered In My Ear.
He Said That He Needed A New Angel,
For Heaven Up Above.
He Came Down To Visit Earth's Garden,
That Is When He Saw You My Love.
God Saw That You Were Weary.
He Knew A Cure Was Not To Be.
So He Took You In His Loving Arms,
He Whispered, Come With Me.
Then He Told Me You Are Blooming Now,
Like His Rose's In His Garden Above,
Now You Were Singing With The Angels,
So Full Of Joy And Love.
God Said You Tried To Stay With Me,
But You Had Too Much Pain.
Though My Heart Is Broken Now,
I Should Not Wish You Back To Suffer Again.
She Is The Loveliest In My Garden Now,
Said God, Just Like A Flower In Bloom,
What She Suffered Here On Earth,
Made Her Petals Fall Too Soon.
I Know You Miss Her So Much,
And I Am Sure She Misses You Too.
One Day In My Paradise,
She Will Meet Up Again With You.
So Now When I See Rose's,
Or Smell Their Sweet Perfume.

I Think Of Her In Gods Heavenly Garden,
So Happy And In Full Bloom.

LONELY PEOPLE

Do You See The Lonely People,
That Are Sitting All Alone.
Each Time That You See Them,
They Are Always On Their Own.
You Often See Them Linger,
And Stand Around Awhile,
Have You Gave Them A Few Words
Or Just Even Gave A Smile.
If You Only Gave A Minute,
Or A Little Bit Of Praise,
I Am Sure You Would Make Them Happy,
Plus Your Spirits It Would Raise.
Just Some Simple Words Of Kindness,
I Am Sure That You Will See,
You Could Help A Lonely Person,
Maybe That Person Could Be Me.

YESTERDAY

My Thoughts Go Back To Yesterday,
With Each Brand New Year I Greet.
It Is Then I Start Remembering,
When My Life Was So Complete.
I Think Of The Special Love We Had,
And All The Dreams I Shared With You.
Now All I Have Are Sweet Memories,
Of You And The Life We Once Knew.
I Did Not Think About Tomorrow,
Now I Realise I Was Wrong.
I Took Our Love For Granted.
Before I Knew Our Time Was Gone.
Now I Know That We Should Live
For Each Moment.
Enjoy Each Minute Until Life Is Through.
Know That God's Plans Are Not Ours.
Maybe Tomorrow Will Not Come For You.
I Know I Should Have Reached For The Stars,
Or At Least Tried To Get The Moon.
Then If I Failed, I Had Tried My Best.
If Time Ran Out Too Soon..
So This New Year Has Started.
I Try And Smile At Every Person I Meet.
I Shed My Tears From A Broken Heart,
When All The World Is Fast Asleep.

A SPECIAL LADY

I Know A Special Lady,
Who Lives Next Door To Me.
A Kinder Sweeter Person.
You Could Ever Wish To See.
She Helped Me Through My Struggles,
Shared All The Good And Bad.
She Is The Best Friend And Neighbour,
That Anyone Ever Had.
We Often Talk About Our Families
For Years She Watched Mine Grow.
When I Went To Her With Worries,
She Helped More Than She Could Know.
We Have Lived Next Door For Years Now,
Alas, We Are Growing Old.
The Memories That I Have Of Her,
Are Worth More To Me Than Gold.
We Have To Be Grateful For What Life Brings,
And Accept What Is Mean't To Be.
I Know Mary And I Will Stays Friends
And Neighbours, For All Eternity.

BEAUTY

So You Really Think You Are Beautiful,
But Are You Beautiful On The Inside.
Do You Often Say You Are Perfect,
Your Heart Knows You Have Lied.
Have You Done Your Best, For The Folk In Need.
Fed The Hungry, Or Led The Blind.
Have You Done Your Bit,for This World Of Ours.
Do You Pray For All Mankiind.
Do You Thank The Lord For All He Gives,
Or Do You Keep On Wanting More.,
If You Want God To Change The Selfish
Way That You Live,
Just Knock And He Will Open The Door.
Then I Am Sure You Will Be Beautiful,
On The Outside, And Deep In Your Soul
Instead Of Feeling Half Alive,
God Will Make Your Life Feel Whole.

LIFE'S RACE

Do You Think Your Life Is Wonderful,
Or Is It In A Mess.
When You Wake Up In The Morning,
Are You Filled With Happiness.
Can You Never Find What You Are Looking For,
Or Maybe You Do Not Care,
Have You Asked The Lord To Help You,
Do You Believe He Is Not There
There Are Many Folk Just Like You,
Always Rushing To Get Things Done.
They Never Hear The Birds Sing,
Never Stop To Feel The Sun.
Why Not Sit Down In A Garden,
Smell The Flowers, And Close Your Eyes.
A Few Minutes Might Turn To Hours,
Perhaps You Will Realise.
Breathe In The Peace This Brings You.
Watch The Birds, And Listen Too.
Hear The Whisper Of The Soft Breeze,
Floating White Clouds In A Sky Of Blue.
Do This Often Or Go On The Seashore,
Feel The Peace All Nature Bring's,
You Will Know God Truely Loves You,
The Way He Loves All Living Things.
Why Not Ask The Lord To Help You,
I Am Certain If You Do,
He Will Free You From Lifes Rat Race,
A Brand New Life Can Start For You.

END OF A RAINBOW

If God Could Grant Me A Miracle,
I Know What It Would Be,
To Let Me Visit Heaven,
Then Bring You Home With Me.
My Poor Heart Is So Broken,
Since The Day You Went Away.
My Skies Are Forever Cloudy,
Everyday Is Dark And Grey.
Lord, I Will Not Need An Angel To Guide Me,
I Think I Know Which Way To Go,
I Will Just Follow The Stars
Along The Milky Way,
Until I Come To The End Of The Rainbow.
Then I Will See You Patiently Waiting,
Standing On Heavens Golden Shore,
I Will Clasp My Arms Around You,
Then I Will Weep For You No More.
God, If This Miracle You Cannot Grant Me,
To Heal This Poor Heart Of Mine,
Then Do The Next Best Thing For Me,
Please Turn Back The Hands Of Time.

BOOK OF MEMORIES

When I Am Feeling Lonely,
Or Feeling Sad And Blue.
I Open My Book Of Memories,
To Remember My Life With You.
My Thoughts Recall The Night We Met,
And The Day That We Were Wed.
You Would Never Leave Me,
You So Often Said.
Then We Had Our First Born,
Our Hearts Were Full Of Pride.
In The Years That Followed,
You Never Left My Side.
Now Our Children Are Grown Up,
And From The Nest Have Flown.
I Never Thought The Day Would Come,
When I Would Be On My Own.
Just When Our Life Was Happiest,
From All Cares And Stress Were Free.
God In His Mysterious Ways,
Took You My Love From Me.
For Time And Tide Wait For No One,
Hard Work Had Taken It's Toil,
I Tried So Hard To Ease Your Pain,
I Prayed To God To Make You Whole.
Then The Angels Came For You,
They Took Away Your Pain.
Now God Has Another Angel,
My Loss Was Heaven's Gain.
One Day I Will See You Standing,
Upon Heaven's Golden Shore.

I Will Hold You In My Arms Again,
And Weep For You No More.
You Know How Much I Miss You,
How Much I Truly Care.
Living Life Without You,
Is Very Hard To Bear.
I Have My Book Of Memories,
From Which I Will Never Part,
I Keep It Safely Locked Away,
It Is Deep Within My Heart.
If My Tears Start To Flow,
Or I Am Sad And Blue.
I Open My Book Of Memories,
To Yesterday And You.

A GENTLEMAN

My Father Was A Rich Man,
In The Things He Did For Others.
He Always Helped His Neighbours Out,
He Classed Everyone As Brothers.
Always Had A Kind Word,
For All The Folk He New,
His Treasures Were His Family,
Plus Good Friends So Warm And True.
He Would Give His Last To Those In Need,
To Us He Gave It All,
He Had No Envy And No Greed,
With Him We All Stood Tall.
I Could Never Be As Good As Him,
I Try To When I Can.
All I Can Say, Is That I Am Proud,
My Dad Was A Gentleman.

MY NANA

My Nana She Was My Best Friend,
Who Mean't The World To Me.
She Gave Me Lots Of Love And Care,
She Left A Beautiful Memory.
She Always Had A Kind Word,
Plus A Smile Upon Her Face..
I Miss Her Love And Tender Touch,
I Miss Her Warm Embrace.
She Taught Me How To Live My Life,
From The Days When I Was Small.
She Taught Me How To Have Respect,
Was There Until I Grew Tall.
I Have Lost My Lovely Nana Now,
But In My Heart She Will Always Be.
She Is Surely An Angel In Heaven,
For My Dear Nana Was An Angel To Me.

JUST THINK

When You Are Feeling Sad,
And You Are Lonely Too.
Just Think Of The People,
Who Are Far Worse Off Than You.
Think Of All The Animals,
That Men Just Kill For Greed.
All Of God's Children,
That No One Will Feed.
Think Of Them All,
In The Flood And The Storm.
Think Of The Homeless,
That Nobody Will Warm.
Plus All Of The Countries,
That Have Been Shattered By War,
With All The Poor Children,
Who Still Carry A Scar.
Think Of These Things,
I Am Sure If You Do,
That You Will Feel Lucky,
This Is Not You.

TO MY DAUGHTER

To My Darling Daughter,
No Words Can Describe,
How Much You Mean To Me,
Except To Say When You Were Born,
I Was In Ecstacy.
From The Moment I First Saw You,
I Knew My Dreams Had All Come True.
With Two Strong Sons Already,
Now I Had A Beautiful Daughter Too.
I Watched You Grow So Quickly,
I Prayed Life Would Be Good To You.
That You Would Find Happiness,
With Strength To See You Through.
I Know That You Are So Happy Now,
You Have What All Are Searching For.
Your Love, And Two Lovely Children,
I Could Not Have Wished For More.
Your Father And I Are Content Now,
We Did Our Best To Help You Through.
You Know How Much We Love And Care,
Now The Rest Is Up To You.
I Hope That When I Am In Heaven,
I Will Be A Lovely Thought In Your Memory.
I Just Want To Say, Thank You,
My Beautiful Daughter,
For Sharing Your Precious
Family With Me.

GOD'S BLESSING

God Gave Me His Sweetest Blessing,
On The Day That You Were Born.
He Sent To Earth An Angel,
I Could Put All My Hopes Upon.
You Gave Me So Much Happiness,
I Pray All Your Dreams Come True.
You Gave Me A Reason For Living,
The Day That Your Mother Had You.
I Have Loved You From A Baby,
I Tenderly Watched You Grow.
Now You Are A Young Women.
This Is What I Want You To Know
That I Will Always Love You,
I Will Care Your Whole Life Too.
When Am Gone, I Will Shout From Heaven,
Natalie, Your Grandma Is So Proud Of You.

PRAYER'S ANSWERED

I Asked God If You Were Happy.
Would He Please Send Me A Sign.
In My Dreams That Night You Told Me,
Not To Worry, You Were Fine.
You Said You Had Met The Good Lord,
Now From Pain And Care Wer'e Free.
You Could Visit Me When You Wanted,
That You Were Never Far From Me.
You Said I Must Stop Weeping,
Not To Grieve So, Or Be Sad,
To Be Grateful For The Good Times,
Forget About The Bad.
You Would Always Love Me,
I Must Still Journey On.
I Felt A Kiss, A Warm Embrace,
When I Awoke You Were Gone.
There Was A Smile Upon My Face,,
God Had Answered To My Prayer.
It Gave Me Hope, I Have No Doubt,
I Believe You Are There.
The Dear Lord, And You Are Both With Me,
I Now Feel That You Are Near
I Can Face Whatever Comes My Way.
With That Life Holds No Fear.

FLOWERS

You Always Gave Me Flowers,
Oh How I Loved Them So.
But I Have Never Had One Flower,
Since The Day You Had To Go.
When I See Them In My Garden,
My Thoughts Go Back To You.
You Often Gave Me Rose's,
A Token Of Our Love So True.
It Is Me Who Gives The Flowers Now,
I Pick A Bunch So Fair,
Then I Wander To Your Resting Place,
I Place Them All With Care.
I Whisper Very Softly,
My Darling I Am Here,
I Spend A Little Time With You,
As I Wipe Away Each Tear.
My Mind Goes Back To Years Ago,
To The Day I Became Your Wife.
The Only Thing I Can Give You
Now My Love, Are Flowers
For The Rest Of My Life.

THANKFUL

When I Wake Up In The Morning,
I Here The Patter Of Tiny Feet.
I Have Never Felt More Happy,
Or My Life Been So Complete.
I See Two Angel Faces,
Peeping Around The Bedroom Door.
This Is What Heaven Must Feel Like,
Having A Family That I Adore.
I Know I Am So Lucky,
To Have My Love, And My Children Too.
Thank You Dear Lord For Making,
All My Dreams Come True.
As I Pray Dear Lord I Ask You,
That My Loved Ones You Will Bless.
Protect Them And Guide Them,
And Give Them Happiness.

MEMORY LANE

There Is A Road I Walk Along,
They Call It Memory Lane.
This Path I Often Wander,
Where I Hear You Call My Name.
Then Together We Walk Hand In Hand,
Until We Reach Our Special Place,
We Sit Awhile On Our Favourite Bench,
Aglow With Love, Time Cannot Erase.
You Say You Will Always Be With Me,
That I Must Stay Strong For You.
Very Few Had What We Have,
A Love So Warm And True.
Our Time Has Gone So Quickly,
It Is Time For Me To Go.
My Heart It Starts To Ache Again,
But As I Walk Away I Know.
That When I Am Feeling Lonely,
When My Heart Starts Breaking In Two.
I Just Take A Walk Down Memory Lane,
Where I Will Meet Again With You.

OUR NEW GRANDAUGHTER

The Angels Are Celebrating, A New Child Is Born.
A New Baby In Our Family,
How Quick Nine Month's Have Flown.
Her Mam And Dad Are So Happy,
Both Her Sibling's Shout With Glee.
Everyone Is So Delighted,
She Has Joined Our Family.
God Has Blessed Us With This Lovely Child,
That We Can Love And Cherish Forever.
She Will Fit Snug Into Our Heart's,
Where We Keep Them All Together.
She Will Bring Us Love, And Bring Us Joy,
I Am Sure That We Will Find,
She Will Be Like All Our Family,
So Beautiful Good And Kind.
Her Grandparents Adore Her Already,
Another Reason For Us To Live On.
A New Baby In Our Family,
To Pin All Our Dreams Upon.
So Our Darling Baby Girl,
We Hope Life Is Good To You, We Wish You Love,
We Wish You Luck, And Good Health We Wish You Too.
We Wish You Joy And Happiness,
That Will Last Your Whole Life Through.
If We Could Grant Just One Wish,
The Thing We Would Give To You,
Is That You Would Have The Love Of God,
To Make All You Dreams Come True.
With Love From Grandma And Granda XXX

TO JESSICA MY SPECIAL ANGEL AGE 6 YEARS

It Six Years Since You Were Born,
How Quick The Times Past By,
Since God Sent Us An Angel,
His Blessing Fron The Sky.
He Gave The Best That He Could Find,
To Pin Our Dreams Upon,
He Asked His Angels In Heaven,
To Pick Us A Special One.
My Heart Lit Up When I Saw Your Face,
Our Own Precious Baby Girl,
My Heart Was Full Of Pride And Joy,
My Head Was In A Whirl.
I Loved You From The Moment,
That I Saw You Lying There.
You Gave Me A Reason For Living,
Knowing Many Of Your Dreams I Would Share.
My Wish As You Blow Out Your Candles,
Is That You, God Will Forever Bless.
You Gave Me Six Years Of Hugs And Kisses,
Plus Lots Of Happiness.
You Gave Me More Than You Will Ever Know,
Just By Being In Our Family,
My Beautiful Little Birthday Girl,
You Mean The World To Grandad And Me.
                                    XXXXXX

BUTTERCUPS

When I See Buttercups,
They Make Me Think Of You.
We Used To Walk In Fields Of Them,
And Parks All Summer Through.
Their Colour Cheers My Heart Up.
I Feel Their Brightness Flow,
I Often Walk In That Same Park,
Where We Would Always Go.
When The Spring Is Here I Miss You,
Same With The Autumn And Winter Too.
But When The Buttercups Appear
In The Summertime.
My Poor Heart Yearns For You.
I See All The Flowers Blooming,
The Bird's Are Singing Too.
So Many Wonderful Memories,
But I Wish I Still Had You.
So I Will Wander In These Fields Of Gold,
On A Warm And Sunny Day,
I Will Imagine You Are Here With Me,
Never Far Away .
If I Close My Eyes, And Pray To God,
Perhaps He Will Hear My Plea.
Instead Of Walking On My Own,
You Are Hand In Hand With Me.

A PLACE IN HEAVEN

I Was Watching This Old World Go By,
Sitting On A Park Bench One Day.
When A Group Of Folk Sat Next To Me,
Then I Heard One Say.
I Wonder If There Is A Heaven?
Where Can Heaven Be?
They Were So Engrossed With This
Topic Of Conversation,
That They Hardly Noticed Me.
I Felt A Raindrop On My Face,
So I Decided I Would Go.
They Were Still Asking This Question,
And If Their Friends Might Know.
If There Really Is A Heaven, She Asked,
How Can I Secure A Place,
Will I Have To Attend Church Or Chapel,
And Sing Amazing Grace.
Perhaps I Might Feed The Hungry,
Then Give All My Wealth Away.
Will I Have To Pray To God Every Single Day?
I Glanced Up At This Lady,
As She Looked At Me, I Smiled And Said,
I Can Tell You, And This Advice I Will Give You
    Free.
I Knew They Might Just Laugh At Me,
But I Decided To Give It A Go,
I Was Having Second Thoughts By Now,
Although They Said They Wanted To Know.
Just Open Up Your Heart I Said,
Then God Can Enter In, You Will Feel

Your Spirit Soar, You Will Feel A Peace Within.
If You Ask The Lord He Will Guide You,
Along Life's Path He Will Lead You Too,
If You Have Love And Kindness In Your Heart,
He Will Have A Lot Of Work For You.
You May Have To Help The Sick And Needy,
Carry The Lame Or Lead The Blind,
Love Your Neighbours And All God's Creatures,
Then I Am Sure That You Will Find.
You Do Not Need To Be A Saint Or A Angel,
Or A Martyr Be, You Will Have Earned
Your Place In Heaven, For All Eternity.

A NEW YEAR

Another Year Has Ended.
How Quick Twelve Months Have Flown,
I Am At My Happiest Now Than I Have Ever
    Known.
My Children Are All Grown Now,
Each Have A Family.
My Heart It Swells With Love And Pride,
They Are All The World To Me.
We Have Had Our Struggles,
Just Tried To Do Our Best,
We Gave Our Children Lots Of Love,
And God He Did The Rest.
I Often Think Of Years Gone By,
With All The Fun We Had,
We Had To Learn To Take The Good Times,
Along With All The Bad.
Now We Have Reached A Milestone,
We Realise That We Are Growing Old,
But I Would Not Change My Life,
For A Million Pounds In Gold.
If God Could Fulfil A Wish For Me,
A Dream That Could Come True,
To See My Grandchildren Strong And Grown,
Perhaps See Their Offspring Too.
I Must Not Be Greedy, I Will Take
What The Lord Gives To Me,
Every New Day Is A Bonus.
What Will Be Is Mean't To Be.

FAVOURITE FLOWERS

My Favourite Flowers Are Rose's,
They Mean A Lot To Me,
And Bring So Many Memories,
Of Days That Used To Be.
You Always Gave Me Rose's,
Any Colour I Did Not Mind,
Now That You Are Not With Me,
I Always Seem To Find.
That When I Pass A Garden,
And See These Flowers In Bloom.
I Feel A Ache Deep In My Heart,
When I Smell Their Sweet Perfume.
It Is Then I Feel You Close To Me,
I Know That You Are Near.
I Think Of How Much I Loved You,
As I Brush Away A Tear.
I Seem To Hear You Whisper,
My Love I Miss You Too.
The Rose's In Heaven Are Beautiful,
I Will Keep A Bunch For You.

HIGHEST PEAK

Have You Climbed Lifes Mountains,
Stood On The Tallest Peak,
Have You Swam Lifes Fastest Rivers,
Do You Protect The Poor And Weak.
Are You Always Giving Out Kind Thoughts,
For Thoughts Are Living Things,
Do You Help The Sick And Needy,
Can You Take Anything This Life Brings.
Do You Believe There Is A Heaven,
A God Who Loves You Too.
No Matter How Rough The Path Is,
You Know God Will Get You Through.
If You Ever Get Stuck On This Bumpy Road,
Can Not Decide Which Path To Choose.,
The Lord Is There With Every Step,
With God You Just Can't Lose.
Everyone Has Free Will,
But If You Need Help In Your Lifes Plan.
Ask God To Lead Your Footsteps,
He Will Make You A Finer Man.
If You Are Still Not Sure Where To Go,
Or Not Know What Road To Seek,
Ask God For Faith And Courage,
You Too Will Scale Lifes Highest Peak.

LIFES ROAD

Do You Wander Down Lifes Highways,
Always Looking For The Right Road.
Do You Need A Friend To Help You,
Carry All Your Heavy Load.
Your Body Was So Weary,
Your Heart Is Tired Too.
You Just Cannot Make Your Mind Up,
And Try And Muddle Through.
You Stumble Down A Pathway,
Where You Have Never Been Before.
You Hear Sweet Voices Singing,
Someone Opens The Church Door,
The People Make You Welcome,
They All Invite You In.
You Have Found The Path You Are Seeking,
Now You Can Let Your Life Begin.

RICHES

Do You Want Fame And Fortune,
Mega Rich You Would Like To Be.
Possess A Yacht And Sports Car,
Or Even Win The Lottery.
Some Say, If You Have Too Much Riches,
From Heaven You Will Be Spurned.
It Is Not How Much Wealth You Have,
It Is How Much You Have Learned.
If Your Heart Has Love And Kindness,
Then You Are Rich Indeed.
If You Have Goodness In Your Soul,
You Have All You Will Ever Need.
I Am Sure It Will Not Matter,
If You Are Rich Or Poor,
Helping Others When They Need It,
Will Get You Into Heaven For Sure.
You Do Not Need To Be A Angel,
Just Try And Do Your Best.
If You Keep Faith In Your Heart,
Then God Will Do The Rest.
He Will Not Care If You Are Famous,
Your Creed, Or The Colour Of Your Skin.
If You Help Your Neighbours Out,
Then God Will Let You In.
You Can Not Take Money With You.
Give Some To God's Children In Need.
Then When You Get To Heaven,
You Will Be Rich Indeed.

THIS WORLD

God Saw This World Was Troubled,
This Earth Was In So Much Pain.
He Knew He Had A Lot To Do,
To Make It Well Again.
The Air Was Filled With Poisons.
All Icebergs Crumbling Too.
God Know's That To Save This World,
Would Depend On Me And You.
The Forests Are Disappearing,
Most Of The Animals Gone.
Men Are Filled With Greed And Hatred,
The Wars Are Raging On.
God Knows The Earth Needs Our Help,
We Can Save It If We Try.
If We Ignore God's Warnings.
We Can Kiss This World Goodbye.

YOU ARE ALWAYS THERE

It Is A Long Time Since I Lost You,
But It Feels Like Yesterday.
This Longing Just To Hold You,
It Never Goe's Away.
My Heart Knows It Still Loves You,
My Eyes Ache To See You Too.
Even When I Am Sleeping,
My Dreams Are All Of You.
If I Could Hold You Again,
Just To Feel Your Warm Embrace,
To Fold My Arms Around You,
To Kiss Your Dear Sweet Face.
My Friends Think I Am Over You,
They Never See Me Weep.
I Shed My Tears From A Broken Heart,
When The World Is Fast Asleep.
I Know I Should Be Grateful,
For The Good Life I Have Had,
The Memories Of The Good Times,
Help To Get Me Through The Bad.
You Will Be With Me Forever,
Somewhere Deep Inside My Heart,
This Is Where I Store Your Memory.
With This I Will Never Part.

HOME AGAIN

It Is A Beautiful Morning,
The Sun Is Shining Bright,
Now That You Have Left Me,
I Feel It Still Is Night.
I Hear The Birds All Singing,
The Children Laugh With Glee.
I See The Flowers Blooming,
So What Is Wrong With Me.
I Feel My Heart Is Breaking,
Because You Had To Go.
Life For Me Has Ended Now.
My Heart Misses You So.
But Wait I Can Hear The Birds Sing,
I Can Feel The Sun And Rain.
My Winter Has Just Turned To Spring,
Now You Are Home Again.

MY SECRET SMILE

I Have A Secret Smile,
That Live's Inside Of Me.
It Often Comes On To My Face,
When I Think How It Used To Be.
Together We Were So Happy,
Now My Heart Longs For You,
You Made Life Complete For Me,
Every Dream We Had Came True.
You Have Not Left Me Lonely,
I Feel Your Presence Everyday.
The Love We Had Between Us,
Death Cannot Take Away.
Sometimes When I Feel Weary,
And Can't Keep Up The Pace,
I Think Of How Much You Loved Me,
Then That Smile Comes To My Face.
Though You Are In Heaven,
I Feel You Are Still Here.
That You Are Not Far From Me,
Sometimes Your Voice I Hear,
Your Memory Is Safely Locked Away,
With It I Will Never Part.
For You And My Secret Smile,
Are Deep Within My Heart.

HEAVEN ON EARTH

I Was Talking To A Man One Day,
Is Age Was Ninety Two.
He Told Me All About His Life,
And Spoke Fondly Of The Friends He New.
I Asked If He Believed In Heaven,
Where Did He Think Heaven Could Be.
This Happened Several Years Ago,
I Still Remember What He Told Me.
Everybody Wants To Go To Heaven He Said,
But No One Wants To Die.
Why Do We Believe That Heaven,
Is Somewhere In The Sky.
Life Is What You Make It,
You Can Have Heaven Here On Earth,
If You Have Love And Kindness,
Respect And A Lot Of Self Worth.
Where There Is War And Hatred,
This Must Be Hell Indeed.
If We Have Goodness In Our Heart,
There Is Nothing More We Need.
We Wonder Why God Let's Wars Happen,
The Lord Gave Us All Free Will.
 If We Ask Him To Help Us,
Our Dreams He Would Fulfil.
To Make A Heaven On This Earth,
Will Depend On Me And You.
If We Love Every Living Thing,
Then This Heaven On Earth Will Come True.

ONE TUESDAY MORNING

It Was On A Tuesday Morning.
I Heard A Song So Sweet.
When I Awoke I Saw An Angel,
Standing At My Feet.
Your Dear Mother Has Gone To Heaven.
We Needed To Ease Her Pain.
She Wanted To Be With Your Father,
Now She Is Well Again.
We Know You Loved Her So Much,
That Is Why We Have Come To You.
We Know Your Heart Is Broken,
So We Want To Comfort You Too.
She Thanks You For The Care You Gave,
You Did Your Very Best.
Her Body Was Tired And Weary,
And Her Soul It Needed Rest.
She New Her Time Was Running Out,
That Her Life Was Nearly Through.
The Hands Of Time Had Stopped For Her,
But She Tried To Stay For You.
She Is Living With Us Angels Now,
At Long Last Her Spirits Free.
She Is In Heaven With Your Dear Father,
Where They Will Spend Eternity.

MY PRAYER

I Asked God To Release Me,
To Free Me From This Pain.
Just To See The Love I Lost,
To Hold Her Once Again.
I Never Got To Say Goodbye,
Or Kiss Her Lovely Face.
I Hurried To Her Bedside,
But God's Angels Won The Race.
They Came Down When I Was Not There,
They Knew I Would Not Let Her Go.
So They Arrived Far Too Soon,
The Reason Now I Know.
For In A Dream God Said To Me,
She Was In Too Much Pain.
The Angels Came And Gave Her Peace,
Now She Is Well Again.
She Lives With Me In Heaven,
With Her Loved Ones Who Had Gone Before.
I Heard Your Prayer, You Will See Her Again,
In Your Dreams Forever More.

A BIT OF ADVICE

Do Not Worry About Riches,
Do Not Grieve Wanting Wealth Untold.
If You Have Good Health And Your Family,
This Is Worth Much More Than Gold.
Do Not Let Anger Spoil A Friendship,
Never Let Greed Destroy Your Soul.
If You Want More Than Your Neighbour,
Do Not Let Envy Defeat Your Goal.
Make Yourself A Better Person,
Let Faith And Truth Invade You Heart.
Never Let A Lie Be Spoken,
Lie's Can Blow Your World Apart.
There Is Much More I Could Tell You,
Just Keep On Going Until The Battles Won.
You Have One Life So Go On Live It.
I Am So Proud Of You My Son.

HEAVEN

I Wonder What Heavens Like,
I Can Only Guess.
They Say Lot's Of Angels Live There,
Full To The Brim With Happiness.
Everyone Is Content In Heaven,
There Is All Peace And Light,
And Never Any Darkness,
All Is Gay And Bright.
They Say That In Heaven,
There Is No Class, No Colour Or Creed.
That When You Get To Paradise,
There Is Nothing That You Need.
You Only Get To Heaven,
If You Have Passed God's Test,
His Heaven Must Be Beautiful,
God Only Picks The Best.
So Strive To Do The Best You Can,
Give No One Hurt Or Pain.
Have No Thoughts Like Hate Or Greed,
Give Instead Of Gain.
Then When Your Life Is Over,
And You Knock On Heavens Door,
The Lord Will Smile, And Let You In,
To Live With Him For Evermore.

DO NOT PRETEND

Do You Know How Much God Loves You.
Maybe You Do Not Even Care.
Can You Feel Him In Your Heart And Soul.
Do You Pretend He Is Not There.
Can You Not Feel Him In The Sunshine,
And In The Gentle Breeze.
He Is In Every Flower,
And In All The Birds And Bees.
Spend Some Moments In Fields Of Green,
Just Sit And Wait Awhile.
The Peace Will Make Your Heart Sing,
The Bird Song Make You Smile.
Breathe In The Air Around You,
Just Slowly Close Your Eyes.
Imagine This Is Heaven,
Then You May Realise.
That Life Is Eternal, Nothing Ever Dies.
Your Heart And Every Living Thing,
You Will Find Will Beat Together,
Me And You, Them And God,
Are Joined By Love Forever.
If You Ever Doubt That God Is There,
Do This Everyday.
Ask The Lord To Give You Proof,
Go On Your Knees And Pray.

GOD'S LOVE

I Ask God If He Loved Me,
His Answer Swiftly Came,
Yes I Love You Dearly,
I Love Everyone The Same.
Lord Do You Love The Sinnners,
Just As Much As You Love Me?
I Have Tried My Best To Be Good And Kind,
From Hate And Greed Stay Free.
Softly God Spoke To Me,
I Do Love Everyone The Same,
Think Of Me As A Shepherd,
Who Know's All His Flock By Name.
Some May Wander Off,
From Life's Straight And Narrow Track,
I Always Go In Search For Them,
To Bring Them Safely Back.
So Do Not Be Down Hearted,
For All My Children I Adore,
The Answer To Your Question Is,
I Could Not Love You More.

A LETTER ON YOUR BIRTHDAY

With Love,
Dear Friend It Is Your Birthday,
We Raise Our Glass To You.
We Just Want To Thank You For,
A Friendship Warm And True.
It Is Your Special Birthday,
I Bet The Years Have Flown.
You Will Have So Many Memories,
Of All The Folk You Have Known.
The Friends You Have Are Many,
That You Made Through The Years.
You Must Have Had A Million Smiles,
And Cried A Million Tears.
All Your Many Friend's Who Love You,
Plus All Your Family Too.
Send You Their Good Wishes,
May All Your Dreams Come True.
We Could Not Count How Many Friends,
That You Helped Through The Years.
You Have Cheered Them In Their Bad Times,
Wiped Away So Many Tears.
Thank You For The Friendship,
That You Always Give.
We Hope We Are Best Of Friends,
As Long As We All Live.
There Are Many Things That We Could Add,
The Laughter, Joy And Tears.
Dear Friend, We Will End By Saying,
Heres To The Next Fifty Years.
      Cheers XXX

FOREVER

I Sat And Watched The Sky Last Night.
I Wondered Where You Are.
I Asked You If You Miss Me,
As I Gazed At The Brightest Star.
Because You Were In It,
My Life Was So Complete.
We Shared Lifes Dreams Together,
Each New Day Gladly Greet.
As A Shadow Eclipsed The Moon,
I Heard You Say So Clear,
I Have Not Left You Sweetheart,
I Am Always Here.
Though You Cannot See Me,
I Have Not Travelled Far.
You Will Easy Find Me,
I Am Wherever You Are.
I Sat And Saw The Dawn Break,
The Sun Was High In The Sky.
Our Love Would Last Forever,
So Special It Could Never Die.

STAR OF HOPE

The Hymn Sweet Star Of Hope,
Brings Teardrops To My Eyes.
It Fills My Heart With Peace,
It Makes Me Realise.
Just How Lucky I Have Been,
Most Of My Dreams Came True.
If You Ask The Lord To Help,
He Will Do The Same For You.
I Have Never Walked Lifes Road Alone,
Even When The Path Was Long.
God Carried Me On His Shoulders,
When I Could Not Journey On.
That Is All I Can Tell You,
Much More I Cannot Say.
Except If God Is With You,
You Will Find The Perfect Day.
So When You Hear This Sweet Hymn,
Let Your Soul Lift Up Like Mine.
May The Love Of God Be In Your Heart,
Until The End Of Time.

YOU WILL WIN

This World Is Waiting Just For You,
To Open Year Heart And Live.
Do You Expect To Always Get,
If You Do Not Want To Give.
There Is So Much Joy To Get From Life,
If You Just Open Your Eyes You Will See,
Contentment Is Not Expensive,
And Happiness Is Free.
Try To Reach Your Goal In Life,
Wear A Smile And Not A Frown.
When Thing's Get Too Much For You,
Pick Yourself Up If You Fall Down.
Keep On Doing This Until You Succeed,
And On Your Feet You Firmly Stand.
Most Folk Have Bad Days,
Everyone Needs A Helping Hand.
You Will Cross Lifes Raging Rivers,
Stand Tall On Lifes Highest Peak.
You Know You Have The Courage,
Never Think That You Are Weak.
Do Not Give Up Keep On Trying,
If You Do Life Will Begin,
Never Think That You Will Lose,
Believe That You Will Win.
So Come On Just Go For It,
What Have You Got To Lose.
If You Get Stuck On The Way,
Ask God To Help You Choose.
Have Faith And You Will Succeed,
Pray For Guidance From Above,

You Have The Most Precious Thing In Life.
That Is Your Familys Love.

A LETTER TO HEAVEN

I Wish I Could Send A Letter,
To You In Heaven Above.
In It I Would Give You All My Prayers,
And Send You All My Love.
I Would Ask If You Were Happy,
If You Were Free From Pain.
I Would Tell You I Would Give The World,
To Have You Back Again.
Have You Seen My Mother And Father?
And The Dear Friends We Once New.
Will You Tell Them That I Miss Them,
My Love I Send Them Too.
I Wish I Could Send This Letter,
But Heaven Has No Address.
So I Will See You In My Dreams Tonight,
And End By Saying God Bless.

YESTERDAY

You Left Me Beautiful Memories,
But I Only Wanted You.
The Dreams That We Were Building,
I Know Will Not Come True.
So Many Times I Needed You,
A Million Times I Cried.
My World Stop Turning For Me,
When You Left My Side.
The Light Went Out Of My Life,
The Day You Went Out Of Mine.
Everyday Is Stormy Weather,
Once It Was All Sunshine.
I Believe You Are In Heaven,
Wher Your Sky Is Forever Blue.
My Heart Keeps On Longing,
For Yesterday And You.

THANKYOU

One Night I Sat And Watched The Moon,
I Wished On A Shooting Star.
You Seemed So Very Close To Me,
Yet You Were So Far.
The Time That I Lost You,
Was On Such A Night Like This.
No Time To Give A Last Embrace,
Or Give A Farewell Kiss.
If I Could See You For A Moment,
I Would Say To You,
Thankyou For The Love You Gave,
For My Beautiful Memories Too.
The Years We Spent Together,
Making My Dreams Come True.
Thankyou Most Of All My Love,
For Simply Being You.

THREE LITTLE WORDS

I Know In This Life We Have Mountains To Climb.
Stormy Oceans To Cross Over Too.
When Life Gets Too Much For Us,
We Try To Muddle Through.
If All You See Are Struggles,
Nothing But Trouble And Strife.
I Know A Way To Conquer Them,
To Ease You Through This Life.
I Know Three Words That Can Help You,
Just Say Them And You Will See.
You Have To Mean Them With All Your Heart,
Those Three Little Words Are God Help Me?
These Words Are Small, But If You Mean Them,
More Impressive Words You Could Not Say.
Just Ask The Lord To Help You,
He Will Take All Your Burdens Away.
Then You Will Climb Lifes Highest Mountain,
Cross Over The Deepest Sea.
Most Of All There Will Be Peace In Your Heart,
For God Can Set You Free.

OPEN YOU EYES

There Are Lots Of Lonely People.
If You Open Your Eyes You Will See.
Many In This World Who Are All Alone,
That Have No Friends And No Family.
Please Give Them A Smile Or A Greeting,
Maybe A Kind Word Or Two.
Open Your Heart As Well As You Eyes,
Do Not Rush Past Them As Most Folk Do.
A Simple Gesture Or A Smile,
May Rebound Back To You Again.
It May Cheer A Lonely Person,
And Bring A Little Sunshine,
Instead Of Lifes Pain.

NO DOUBT

My Mother Was So Beautiful,
On The Inside As Well As Out.
She Believed In God With All Her Heart,
My Mother Never Had One Doubt.
She Often Used To Tell Me,
The Best Advice I Can Give To You,
When You Are Sad And Troubled,
Ask The Good Lord To Help You Through.
He Will Never Ignore You,
God Will Ease You Past Your Pain.
He Will Plant Faith In Your Heart Forever,
You Will Never Doubt Again.
My Dear Mother Is Now In Heaven,
But I Still Remember What She Told Me.
In My Prayers I Ask God To Make Me,
Just As Good And Kind As She.

GOD LOVES US ALL

No Other Person Looks Like You,
No One Is The Same Shape Or Size.
Nobody Else In This Whole Wide World,
Has Your Face Or Your Eyes.
God Doe's Not Care If We Are Different,
He Loves Everyone The Same.
Just Think Of Him As A Shepherd,
Who Knows All His Flock By Name.
God Knows Everything About Us,
He Is With Us From Lifes Start.
He Know's If We Are Happy,
Or Have A Broken Heart.
God Can Tell If We Have Told The Truth,
He Knows When We Have Lied.
Is Aware When We Are Suffering,
If We Have Laughed Or Cried.
So Believe In Him With All Your Heart,
Let God Plant Faith In Your Soul.
Then You Will Reap What You Have Sown,
Let Happiness Be Your Goal.

JOURNEY'S END

Do You Wander Lifes Road To Nowhere.
Do You Know The Best Route To Take.
Have You Planned Where You Are Heading.
Maybe You Leave It All To Fate.
Is Your Pathway Steep And Rocky,
Are You Searching High And Low,
For The Best Road To Your Destination,
God Will Show You The Way To Go.
If You Ask Him He Will Guide You,
Along Lifs Straight And Narrow Track.
You May Stray But God Will Find You,
He Will Bring You Safely Back.
It Is Your Choice What Road You Walk On,
And What Speed You Want To Go.
God Will Never Fail You,
In The Fast Lane Or The Slow.
God Will Be Your Driver,
Steer You Past All Doubt And Sin.
Take His Hand The Lord Will Guide You,
Do Not Let The Devil Win.
He Will Stay With You On Lifes Travels.
You Will Never Find A Better Friend.
The Lord Will Love You And Protect You,
Right To Your Journeys End.

GOD PICKED YOU

God Came Down To Visit Earths Garden.
To Pick A Flower Or Two.
When He Saw Your Beauty,
The Dear Lord Picked You Too.
He Saw You Were Tired And Weary,
You Had Suffered Too Much Pain.
He Would Take You To His Heaven,
There You Would Be Well Again.
God Would Put You In His Garden,
Where Only His Best Rose's Grow.
You Will Always Bloom In Sunshine,
Where God's Light And Love All Flow.
When It Is My Time To Take This Journey,
God Might Come And Pick Me Too.
Then I Will Enter God's Beautiful Garden,
Where I Will Bloom Again With You.

ASK GOD

Most Of Us Have Problems.
With A Lot Of Stress And Strain.
Some Carry Heavy Burdens,
Others Are Racked With Guilt And Pain.
A Good Few Have Found The Answer,
Who Seem To Sail Through Life.
You Wonder How They Do It,
When You Are Loaded Down With Strife.
Perhaps They Have A Dear Friend,
Whose Shoulder They Lean Upon,
He Helps Carry Their Worries,
So They Can Soldier On.
Then Maybe They Have This Same Friend,
That Can Bring Peace Into Their Heart.
If You Are Wanting What They Have,
I Will Advise You How To Start.
Sit Somewhere Quiet In A Garden,
Or By A Stream In The Countryside.
Open Your Heart And Ask Him,
If He Will Be Your Guide.
If God Thinks You Really Mean It,
He Will Be Your Best Friend Too.
Ask Him For Faith And Courage,
His Love Will Get You Through.
God Can Give What You Are Seeking,
The Prize All Want To Possess.
With Him In Your Life,you Will Find It,
God Will Give You Happiness.

DOUBTING THOMAS

I Am Defenitely A Doubting Thomas.
I Have Been So From The Start,
I Am Almost Certain That Heaven Exists,
But A Small Doubt Is In My Heart.
I Wish I Could See An Angel,
Standing There With Sparkling Wings.
It Would Be The Icing On The Cake,
I Could Take Anything This Life Brings.
My Life Would Change In That Moment,
All My Doubts Would Fade Away.
I Would Know God Thinks I Am So Special,
That He Sent Me An Angel One Day.
Perhaps Its Peace Would Surround Me.
Praising God With The Songs That It Sings,
They Say Angels Have Beautiful Faces,
Aglow Like Their Shining Wings.
If The Lord Would Grant Me This Blessing,
And A Message Of Joy I Receive.
I Would Be A Hundred Per Cent Certain,
And My Heart Would Surely Believe.

SWEET MEMORIES

Do You Look At The Sky At Night.
Perhaps Wish On The Brightest Star,
You Always Feel So Close To Him,
Yet He Seems So Far.
Then Your Gaze May Wander,
As You Look Towards The Moon.
Your Thoughts Go Back To Years Long Past,
To The Love You Lost Too Soon.
But You Know That You Were Fortunate,
To Have Had A Love Like This.
He Left You With A Beautiful Memory,
And Sweet Memories Are Bliss.

SMILE AGAIN

Life Is What You Make It,
That Is What People Say.
Some Lives Are Filled With Sunshine,
They Look Forward To Each New Day.
Others Have Lives Like Bad Weather,
They Never See Skies That Are Blue.
Is God In Your Life, Or Is He Absent.
Then I Will Tell You What To Do.
Grab This Life By Both Hands,
Do Not Lock Yourself Away.
You Have So Much To Live For,
Keep Seeking That Perfect Day.
Life Goes Over So Quickly,
The Years Go Flying Past.
Do You Feel That Life Is Pointless,
With No Last Straw To Grasp.
Have You A Small Space In Your Heart,
Where God Can Just Squeeze In,
He Will Heal The Gap In Your Soul,
You Will Feel A Peace Within.
He Will Warm You With His Sunshine,
Will Ease Your Hurt And Your Pain.
If You Ask God Into Your Life,
You Will Start To Live Again.
God Will Always Give You Blue Skies,
No More Crying In The Rain.
He Will Banish Every Teardrop,
Then You Will Start To Smile Again.

TELL HIM

Tell God Your Poor Heart Is Broken,
Everyday You Feel Its Pain.
You Need To Hold Her In Your Arms,
And See Her Sweet Face Again.
Tell Him You Are So Lonely,
Now That Your Love Is Gone.
If You Knew She Was Near You,
You Could Still Journey On.
Then Wait For God To Answer,
He Might Tell You In Your Dreams.
That Your Love Is Always With You,
No Matter How Far She Seems.
Just Believe That She Is Happy,
At Peace And Missing You Too.
One Day At Heavens Doorway,
She Will Be There To Welcome You.

PRICELESS

Do You Often Wonder,
What This Life Is All About.
Has It Any Purpose,
Doe's Your Heart Still Doubt.
Have You Got Faith And Solace,
Deep Within Your Soul.
Do You Have No Aim In Life,
Have You Lost Control.
Do You Think In This Vast Universe,
That You Matter Less And Less.
Feel That You Are Not Worthy,
Of Ever Finding Happiness.
Try Watching The Sunset Disappear,
While Sitting By A Lake.
Gaze At The Twinkling Stars At Night.,
Watch A New Dawn Break.
Stroll In The Countryside,
Paddle In A Stream,
Laze In The Garden,
You Might Begin To Dream.
Then You May Come To Realise,
That Every Thing Is One.
This World And All That Is In It,
Lives Forever And Goes On And On.
If You Convince Yourself Of This,
You Might Find Happiness.
To God You Are Special,
In Fact You Are Priceless.

MY DREAM

I Had A Dream The Other Night,
That I Was In Heaven With You.
We Were Walking In Fields Of Corn,
Under A Beautiful Sky Of Blue.
I Met My Dear Mother And Father,
Many Friends That I Once Knew.
They Look So Well And Happy,
In Their Arms I Quickly Flew.
As We Neared An Open Gate,
I New If I Walked Through,
That My Dream Would Be Over,
I Would Say Farewell To You.
They Said That I Was Too Early,
My Heart Wanted So Much To Stay.
I Know You Will Be Waiting,
At Heavens Gate For Me One Day.

ANGEL ON YOUR SHOULDER

There Is An Angel On Your Shoulder,
Someone Told Me This One Day.
Forever There In Lifes Bright Sunshine,
Comforts You When Skies Are Grey.
Your Angel Will Not Leave You,
It Has Been With You From Your Birth.
Followed You On Lifes Journey,
Until It Is Time To Leave This Earth.
Angels Do Their Best To Guide You,
They Know You Have Free Will.
It Will Never Force You,
They Try Their Best To Instil,
Love And Kindness In Your Heart,
Plant God's Faith Deep In Your Soul.
Help You Through Your Problems,
Until You Finally Reach Your Goal.
Most Folk Never See Their Angel,
Perhaps When You Are In Despair.
You Might Feel Them On Your Shoulder,
Your Guardian Angels Always There.

DREAMS COME TRUE

Do You Have God's Peace In Your Heart,
His Calmness In Your Soul.
Is Your Life A War Zone,
Or Are You In Control.
God Can Be Your Confidant,
Your Troubles He Will Share.
The Lord Will Be Your Partner,
Who Will Go With You Everywhere.
If You Want The Peace He Brings You,
That All Are Searching For.
With God Always At Your Shoulder,
You Could Not Want For More.
So Take A Deep Breath And Ask Him,
You May Not Get The Chance Again,
You Can Bathe In God's Bright Sunshine,
Or Choose The Gloom And Rain.
God Is There Just For The Asking,
My Friend It Is Up To You.
You Can Ignore Him If You Want To,
Or Make All Your Dreams Come True.

KNOCK ON HEAVEN'S DOOR

When Your Life Is Over,
And You Knock On Heavens Door.
Will The Lord Let You In,
With Him Forever More.
Will The Good Lord Open It,
Then Sadly Shake His Head,
And Say You Cannot Enter Heaven,
Try The Door Below Instead.
Do Your Best To Make God Smile,
By Aiding The Folk In Need.
Is There Kindness In Your Heart,
Or Is It Filled With Greed.
How Many Friends Have You Made,
That You Can Depend Upon,
How Many Years Have You Lived,
Just Thinking Of Number One.
God Knows The Good Deeds That You Did,
Plus Those You Should Have Done.
The Few Things That You Did Right,
And The Many You Did Wrong.
Change Your Life While You Still Have Time,
Then When You Knock On Heavens Door.
God Will Nod And Let You In,
To Live With Him Forever More.

WHAT IS LOVE

What Is Love, What Is This Thing You Cannot See
    But Feel Very Much.
There Are Many Loves We Can Have In One
    Lifetime.
We All Know The Love We Feel For Our Mothers,
    Our First Love.
Mostly. Me Included Take This Love For Granted.
Until The Day Comes When We Lose Her And She
    Passes Into Spirit.
Then We Would Give Anything, Just To See Her
    Face Or Hold Her Hand
For A Moment, And Hope She New How Much She
    Was Loved.
Another Love Is The Love We Feel For Our Partner,
The One We Plan To Share Our Life With.
The Joys And Sorrows, The Ups And Downs This
    Life Brings.
We Think That We Will Grow Old Together, But
    Sometimes God's Plans
Are Not Ours, And One Is Left Behind.
If We Did Not Tell Them How Much They Mean't
    To Us While They Were Here,
We Will Regret This, And Never Get The Chance
    Again Until We Too
Pass Into Spirit And Join Them.
The Love That We Feel For Our Children Cannot Be
    Matched,
It Is By Far The Strongest, I Would Gladly Die For
    Any Of Mine, I
Suppose That Most Mothers Would Do The Same.

They Are Many Other Loves, The Love For Our Jobs, For Our Pets,
Our Friends And Neighbours To Name But A Few.
Lastly But Not Least Is The Love We Feel For God,
This Love Has Ebbed And Flowed In My Life, Sometimes Doubting Him
When Things Went Wrong, Forgetting Him When Things Were Great.
Sometimes I Searched For Him In Different Churches, Wanting Proof,
All The Time He Was Right Next To Me In Every Step I Took, And Through
My Busy Life Waited Patiently For Me Until I Was Ready To Ask For Him.
My Favourite Lines In The Bible Are, The Lord Loves You, And Brings
You The Peace That Passes All Understanding.
Truer Words I Have Never Heard,
So What Is This Thing You Cannot See But Feel So Strongly.
I Have Found It To Be The Most Important Gift You Can Have.
If You Have Love You Can Get Through Anything.
I Once Heard Of A Woman Who Had Lost Her Husband And Two Son's
Each After Another, And She Thought She Had Nothing To Live For.
After Some Years Like This She Thought She Would Never Feel Happy Again. Then One Day While Doing The Dishes In The Kitchen, She Looked Out Of The Window Into The Garden, And Saw A Mother Bird Feeding Its Young,

She Could Not Help Smile At The Antics Of The
Baby Birds,
And Their Mother Patiently Feeding Them.
She Realised That If She Could Smile And Get
Pleasure From This,
She Was Not Dead Inside, And Could Still Feel
Love.
She Started Helping Others Who Had Also Suffered
Loss.
So For The Rest Of My Life I Hope This Is A Gift I
Will Always Have.
Money And Wealth We Cannot Take With Us
When We Pass On To Heaven,
But Love We Can Keep Forever.

With Love XXX

ABOUT THE AUTHOR

I am now retired, and I live content with my husband, who I have been married to for forty two years. Our three children are grown with family's of there own. I now have time to do the things that I am interested in. Before with a family to raise and always doing part time work to help out our budget, I did not have much time for anything that did not include my family. Now that my children have flown the nest, I have found time for the things I could not fit in before.

I have always wondered what this life is all about, why we are here? Is there another life after this one? So I decided to find out. I tried different church's, seeking the answer. When I lost my dear mother some years ago I went to a spiritualist church. I am not a person that is easily lead I wanted my own proof, not someone else's. One night at a church meeting I attend. A lady told me that my mother was there with her I was not satisfied with this, then she said that my mother had a name like a plant or flower, that I had some of her hair in a locket that I had left at home, which was true and my mothers name was lily. Now years later I too have developed this gift, and have heard and seen spirit many times myself, Now at long last, I found my answer. xxx